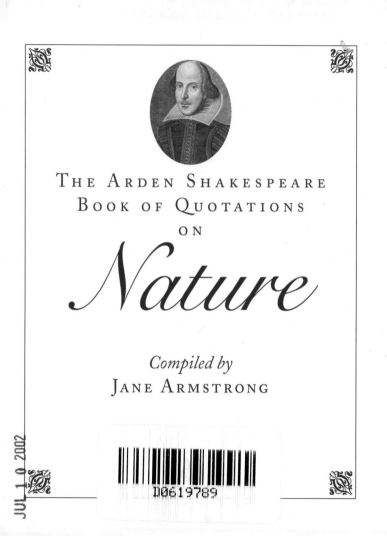

THE ARDEN SHAKESPEARE
BOOK OF QUOTATIONS
ON

Nature

Compiled by
JANE ARMSTRONG

The Arden website is at
http://www.ardenshakespeare.com

First published 2001 by The Arden Shakespeare

This Collection Copyright © 2001 Jane Armstrong

Arden Shakespeare is an imprint of Thomson Learning

Thomson Learning
Berkshire House
168–173 High Holborn
London WC1V 7AA

Designed and typeset by Martin Bristow

Printed in Singapore by Seng Lee Press

British Library Cataloguing in Publication Data
A catalogue record for this book is available from the
British Library

Library of Congress Cataloguing in Publication Data
A catalogue record has been requested

ISBN 1-903436-55-9

NPN 9 8 7 6 5 4 3 2 1

Nature

THE ARDEN SHAKESPEARE
BOOKS OF QUOTATIONS

Life

Love

Death

Nature

Songs & Sonnets

The Seven Ages of Man

The Natural World

In nature's infinite book of secrecy
A little I can read.

Antony and Cleopatra 1.2.10–11

Naught so vile that on the earth doth live
But to the earth some special good doth give;
Nor aught so good but, strained from that fair use,
Revolts from true birth, stumbling on abuse.

Romeo and Juliet 2.3.13–16

❧

Mickle is the powerful grace that lies
In plants, herbs, stones, and their true qualities.

Romeo and Juliet 2.3.11–12

The Seasons

How many things by season, seasoned are
To their right praise, and true perfection!

Merchant of Venice 5.1.107–8

The seasons alter: hoary-headed frosts
Fall in the fresh lap of the crimson rose;
And on old Hiems' thin and icy crown,
An odorous chaplet of sweet summer buds
Is, as in mockery, set; the spring, the summer,
The childing autumn, angry winter, change
Their wonted liveries.

Midsummer Night's Dream 2.1.107–13

SPRING

When daisies pied and violets blue
 And lady-smocks all silver-white
And cuckoo-buds of yellow hue
 Do paint the meadows with delight,
The cuckoo then on every tree
Mocks married men; for thus sings he:
    'Cuckoo!
Cuckoo, cuckoo!' O, word of fear,
Unpleasing to a married ear.

When shepherds pipe on oaten straws
 And merry larks are ploughmen's clocks,
When turtles tread and rooks and daws,
 And maidens bleach their summer smocks,
The cuckoo then, on every tree,
Mocks married men; for thus sings he:
    'Cuckoo!
Cuckoo, cuckoo!' O, word of fear,
Unpleasing to a married ear.

Love's Labour's Lost 5.2.885–902

From you have I been absent in the spring,
When proud pied April, dressed in all his trim,
Hath put a spirit of youth in everything.

Sonnet 98

❀

It was a lover and his lass,
    With a hey and a ho and a hey nonino,
That o'er the green corn-field did pass,
    In spring-time, the only pretty ring-time,
When birds do sing, hey ding a ding, ding,
Sweet lovers love the spring.

Between the acres of the rye,
    With a hey and a ho and a hey nonino,
These pretty country-folks would lie,
    In spring-time, the only pretty ring-time,
When birds do sing, hey ding a ding, ding,
Sweet lovers love the spring.

This carol they began that hour,
    With a hey and a ho and a hey nonino,
How that a life was but a flower,
    In spring-time, the only pretty ring-time,
When birds do sing, hey ding a ding, ding,
Sweet lovers love the spring.

And therefore take the present time,
    With a hey and a ho and a hey nonino,
For love is crowned with the prime,
    In spring-time, the only pretty ring-time,
When birds do sing, hey ding a ding, ding,
Sweet lovers love the spring.

As You Like It 5.3.15–38

❀

When daffodils begin to peer,
    With heigh! the doxy over the dale,
Why then comes in the sweet o' the year,
    For the red blood reigns in the winter's pale.

Winter's Tale 4.3.1–4

Primrose, first-born child of Ver,
Merry springtime's harbinger,
   With harebells dim.
Oxlips in their cradles growing,
Marigolds on deathbeds blowing,
   Lark's-heels trim.

Two Noble Kinsmen 1.1.7–12

❀

   Daffodils,
That come before the swallow dares, and take
The winds of March with beauty, violets, dim,
But sweeter than the lids of Juno's eyes
Or Cytherea's breath; pale primroses,
That die unmarried, ere they can behold
Bright Phoebus in his strength . . . bold oxlips and
The crown imperial; lilies of all kinds,
The flower-de-luce being one.

Winter's Tale 4.4.118–27

Summer

Under the greenwood tree,
    Who loves to lie with me,
And turn his merry note
    Unto the sweet bird's throat,
Come hither, come hither, come hither.
    Here shall he see
    No enemy,
But winter and rough weather.

Who doth ambition shun,
    And loves to live i' th' sun,
Seeking the food he eats,
    And pleased with what he gets,
Come hither, come hither, come hither.
    Here shall he see
    No enemy,
But winter and rough weather.

As You Like It 2.5.1–8, 35–42

As full of spirit as the month of May,
And gorgeous as the sun at midsummer.

1 Henry IV 4.1.101–2

❧

Shall I compare thee to a summer's day?
Thou art more lovely and more temperate:
Rough winds do shake the darling buds of May,
And summer's lease hath all too short a date:
Sometime too hot the eye of heaven shines,
And often is his gold complexion dimmed;
And every fair from fair sometime declines,
By chance, or nature's changing course, untrimmed:
But thy eternal summer shall not fade,
Nor lose possession of that fair thou ow'st,
Nor shall death brag thou wander'st in his shade,
When in eternal lines to time thou grow'st:
    So long as men can breathe or eyes can see,
    So long lives this, and this gives life to thee.

Sonnet 18

The fairest flowers o'th' season
Are our carnations and streaked gillyvors . . .
Hot lavender, mints, savory, marjoram,
The marigold, that goes to bed wi'th' sun
And with him rises, weeping.

Winter's Tale 4.4.81–2, 104–6

❦

Where the bee sucks, there suck I:
In a cowslip's bell I lie;
There I couch when owls do cry.
On the bat's back I do fly
After summer merrily.
Merrily, merrily, shall I live now,
Under the blossom that hangs on the bough.

Tempest 5.1.88–94

Love, whose month is ever May.

Love's Labour's Lost 4.3.99

Now these hot days is the mad blood stirring.

Romeo and Juliet 3.1.4

Why, this is very midsummer madness.

Twelfth Night 3.4.56

More matter for a May morning!

Twelfth Night 3.4.142

Autumn

The teeming autumn big with rich increase.

Sonnet 97

Expect Saint Martin's summer, halcyon's days.

1 Henry VI 1.2.131

Earth's increase, foison plenty,
Barns and garners never empty.
Vines with clustering bunches growing,
Plants with goodly burden bowing;
Spring come to you at the farthest,
In the very end of harvest.

Tempest 4.1.110–15

When lofty trees I see barren of leaves,
Which erst from heat did canopy the herd,
And summer's green all girded up in sheaves,
Borne on the bier with white and bristly beard:
Then of thy beauty do I question make,
That thou among the wastes of time must go,
Since sweets and beauties do themselves forsake,
And die as fast as they see others grow.

Sonnet 12

❋

As wild geese that the creeping fowler eye,
Or russet-pated choughs, many in sort,
Rising and cawing at the gun's report,
Sever themselves, and madly sweep the sky.

Midsummer Night's Dream 3.2.20–3

❋

Leaves look pale, dreading the winter's near.

Sonnet 97

[16]

WINTER

When icicles hang by the wall
    And Dick the shepherd blows his nail
And Tom bears logs into the hall
    And milk comes frozen home in pail,
When blood is nipped and ways be foul,
Then nightly sings the staring owl:
                'Tu-whit, Tu-whoo!'
A merry note,
While greasy Joan doth keel the pot.

When all aloud the wind doth blow
    And coughing drowns the parson's saw
And birds sit brooding in the snow
    And Marian's nose looks red and raw,
When roasted crabs hiss in the bowl,
Then nightly sings the staring owl:
                'Tu-whit; Tu-whoo!'
A merry note,
While greasy Joan doth keel the pot.

Love's Labour's Lost 5.2.903–20

Winter tames man, woman, and beast.

Taming of the Shrew 4.1.21

That time of year thou mayst in me behold,
When yellow leaves, or none, or few do hang
Upon those boughs which shake against the cold,
Bare ruined choirs where late the sweet birds sang;
In me thou seest the twilight of such day
As after sunset fadeth in the west,
Which by and by black night doth take away,
Death's second self that seals up all in rest.

Sonnet 73

Sap checked with frost and lusty leaves quite gone,
Beauty o'er-snowed and bareness everywhere.

Sonnet 5

Blow, blow, thou winter wind,
Thou art not so unkind
   As man's ingratitude.
Thy tooth is not so keen,
Because thou art not seen,
   Although thy breath be rude.
Heigh-ho, sing heigh-ho, unto the green holly
Most friendship is feigning, most loving mere folly.
Then heigh-ho, the holly,
   This life is most jolly.

Freeze, freeze, thou bitter sky,
That dost not bite so nigh
   As benefits forgot.
Though thou the waters warp,
Thy sting is not so sharp,
   As friend remembered not.
Heigh-ho, sing heigh-ho, unto the green holly
Most friendship is feigning, most loving mere folly.
Then heigh-ho, the holly,
   This life is most jolly.

As You Like It 2.7.174–93

After summer evermore succeeds
Barren winter, with his wrathful nipping cold.

2 Henry VI 2.4.2–3

This place is too cold for Hell.

Macbeth 2.3.16–17

'Tis bitter cold,
And I am sick at heart.

Hamlet 1.1.8–9

HAMLET The air bites shrewdly, it is very cold.
HORATIO It is a nipping and an eager air.

Hamlet 1.4.1–2

A killing frost.

Henry VIII 3.2.355

❊

This is a brave night to cool a courtesan.

King Lear 3.2.78

❊

Winter's not gone yet, if the wild geese fly that way.

King Lear 2.2.239–40

❊

How like a winter hath my absence been
From thee, the pleasure of the fleeting year!
What freezings have I felt, what dark days seen,
What old December's bareness everywhere!

Sonnet 97

At Christmas I no more desire a rose
Than wish a snow in May's newfangled shows,
But like of each thing that in season grows.

Love's Labour's Lost 1.1.105–7

❄

Some say that ever 'gainst that season comes
Wherein our Saviour's birth is celebrated,
This bird of dawning singeth all night long;
And then, they say, no spirit dare stir abroad,
The nights are wholesome, then no planets strike,
No fairy takes, nor witch hath power to charm,
So hallowed and so gracious is that time.

Hamlet 1.1.163–9

Day into Night

MORNING

Night's swift dragons cut the clouds full fast;
And yonder shines Aurora's harbinger,
At whose approach, ghosts wandering here and there
Troop home to churchyards. Damned spirits all,
That in cross-ways and floods have burial,
Already to their wormy beds are gone.

Midsummer Night's Dream 3.2.379–84

❀

      The morning's war,
When dying clouds contend with growing light,
What time the shepherd, blowing of his nails,
Can neither call it perfect day nor night.

3 Henry VI 2.5.1–4

But look, the morn in russet mantle clad
Walks o'er the dew of yon high eastward hill.

Hamlet 1.1.171–2

The grey-eyed morn smiles on the frowning night,
Chequering the eastern clouds with streaks of light;
And darkness fleckled like a drunkard reels
From forth day's pathway, made by Titan's wheels.

Romeo and Juliet 2.2.188–91

The country cocks do crow, the clocks do toll.

Henry V 4.0.15, on the morning of the battle
of Agincourt

JULIET Wilt thou be gone? It is not yet near day.
It was the nightingale and not the lark
That pierced the fearful hollow of thine ear.
Nightly she sings on yond pomegranate tree.
Believe me, love, it was the nightingale.
ROMEO It was the lark, the herald of the morn,
No nightingale. Look, love, what envious streaks
Do lace the severing clouds in yonder east.
Night's candles are burnt out, and jocund day
Stands tiptoe on the misty mountain tops.

Romeo and Juliet 3.5.1–10

❖

But soft, methinks I scent the morning air.

Hamlet 1.5.58

Hark, hark, the lark at heaven's gate sings,
    And Phoebus gins arise,
His steeds to water at those springs
    On chaliced flowers that lies;
And winking Mary-buds begin to ope their golden eyes;
With every thing that pretty is, my lady sweet arise:
    Arise, arise!

Cymbeline 2.3.20–6

❁

The lark at break of day arising,
From sullen earth sings hymns at heaven's gate.

Sonnet 29

❁

Fairy king, attend and mark:
I do hear the morning lark.

Midsummer Night's Dream 4.1.92–3

Full many a glorious morning have I seen
Flatter the mountain tops with sovereign eye,
Kissing with golden face the meadows green,
Gilding pale streams with heavenly alchemy;
Anon permit the basest clouds to ride
With ugly rack on his celestial face.

Sonnet 33

The golden sun salutes the morn
And, having gilt the ocean with his beams,
Gallops the zodiac in his glistering coach
And overlooks the highest-peering hills.

Titus Andronicus 1.1.504–7

Like a red morn that ever yet betokened
Wrack to the seaman, tempest to the field,
    Sorrow to shepherds, woe unto the birds,
    Gusts and foul flaws to herdmen and to herds.

Venus and Adonis 453–6

    The morning, from whose silver breast
The sun ariseth in his majesty;
    Who doth the world so gloriously behold
    That cedar tops and hills seem burnished gold.

Venus and Adonis 855–8

Evening

The west yet glimmers with some streaks of day;
Now spurs the lated traveller apace,
To gain the timely inn.

Macbeth 3.3.5–7

❀

Light thickens; and the crow
Makes wing to th' rooky wood.

Macbeth 3.2.50–1

NIGHT

Swift, swift, you dragons of the night.

Cymbeline 2.2.48

How sweet the moonlight sleeps upon this bank!
Here will we sit, and let the sounds of music
Creep in our ears – soft stillness and the night
Become the touches of sweet harmony:
Sit Jessica, – look how the floor of heaven
Is thick inlaid with patens of bright gold,
There's not the smallest orb which thou behold'st
But in his motion like an angel sings,
Still quiring to the young-eyed cherubins;
Such harmony is in immortal souls,
But whilst this muddy vesture of decay
Doth grossly close it in, we cannot hear it.

Merchant of Venice 5.1.54–65

Peace! – how the moon sleeps with Endymion.

Merchant of Venice 5.1.109

How silver-sweet sound lovers' tongues by night,
Like softest music to attending ears.

Romeo and Juliet 2.2.165–6

Spread thy close curtain, love-performing night,
That runaway's eyes may wink, and Romeo
Leap to these arms untalked-of and unseen.

Romeo and Juliet 3.2.5–7

'In night,' quoth she, 'desire sees best of all.'

Venus and Adonis 720

Ill met by moonlight, proud Titania.

Midsummer Night's Dream 2.1.60

Now entertain conjecture of a time
When creeping murmur and the poring dark
Fills the wide vessel of the universe.

Henry V 4.0.1–3

The gaudy, blabbing and remorseful day
Is crept into the bosom of the sea;
And now loud-howling wolves arouse the jades
That drag the tragic melancholy night,
Who with their drowsy, slow and flagging wings
Clip dead men's graves and from their misty jaws
Breathe foul contagious darkness in the air.

2 Henry VI 4.1.1–7

There's husbandry in heaven;
Their candles are all out.

Macbeth 2.1.4–5

❀

Ere the bat hath flown
His cloistered flight; ere to black Hecate's summons
The shard-born beetle, with his drowsy hums,
Hath rung Night's yawning peal, there shall be done
A deed of dreadful note.

Macbeth 3.2.40–4

❀

'Tis now the very witching time of night.
When churchyards yawn and hell itself breathes out
Contagion to this world.

Hamlet 3.2.390–2

Now the hungry lion roars,
And the wolf behowls the moon;
Whilst the heavy ploughman snores,
All with weary task fordone.
Now the wasted brands do glow,
Whilst the screech-owl, screeching loud,
Puts the wretch that lies in woe
In remembrance of a shroud.
Now it is the time of night
That the graves, all gaping wide,
Every one lets forth his sprite
In the church-way paths to glide.
And we fairies, that do run . . .
Following darkness like a dream,
Now are frolic; not a mouse
Shall disturb this hallowed house.
I am sent with broom before
To sweep the dust behind the door.

Midsummer Night's Dream 5.1.365–84

Stormy Weather

These late eclipses in the sun and moon portend
no good to us.

King Lear 1.2.103–4

The ox hath therefore stretched his yoke in vain,
The ploughman lost his sweat, and the green corn
Hath rotted ere his youth attained a beard;
The fold stands empty in the drowned field,
And crows are fatted with the murrion flock;
The nine-men's-morris is filled up with mud,
And the quaint mazes in the wanton green
For lack of tread are undistinguishable.

Midsummer Night's Dream 2.1.93–100

The earth that's nature's mother is her tomb.

Romeo and Juliet 2.3.5

❀

My flocks feed not, my ewes breed not,
My rams speed not, all is amiss . . .
Clear wells spring not, sweet birds sing not,
Green plants bring not forth their dye.

Passionate Pilgrim 17.1–2, 25–6

❀

You have fed upon my signories,
Disparked my parks and felled my forest woods.

Richard II 3.1.22–3

Things that love night
Love not such nights as these. The wrathful skies
Gallow the very wanderers of the dark,
And make them keep their caves.

King Lear 3.2.42–5

The night has been unruly: where we lay,
Our chimneys were blown down; and, as they say,
Lamentings heard i'th' air; strange screams of death,
And, prophesying with accents terrible
Of dire combustion, and confused events,
New hatched to th' woeful time, the obscure bird
Clamoured the livelong night: some say, the earth
Was feverous, and did shake.

Macbeth 2.3.54–61

So foul and fair a day I have not seen.

Macbeth 1.3.38

The storm is up, and all is on the hazard.

Julius Caesar 5.1.67

Blow winds and crack your cheeks! Rage, blow!
You cataracts and hurricanoes, spout
Till you have drenched our steeples, drowned the cocks!
You sulphurous and thought-executing fires,
Vaunt-couriers of oak-cleaving thunderbolts,
Singe my white head! And thou, all-shaking thunder,
Strike flat the thick rotundity o'the world,
Crack nature's moulds, all germens spill at once
That make ingrateful man!

King Lear 3.2.1–9

A Seascape

How fearful
And dizzy 'tis to cast one's eyes so low.
The crows and choughs that wing the midway air
Show scarce so gross as beetles. Half-way down
Hangs one that gathers samphire, dreadful trade;
Methinks he seems no bigger than his head.
The fishermen that walk upon the beach
Appear like mice, and yon tall anchoring barque
Diminished to her cock, her cock a buoy
Almost too small for sight. The murmuring surge
That on th'unnumbered idle pebble chafes,
Cannot be heard so high.

King Lear 4.6.11–22

Words for Gardeners

Now 'tis the spring, and weeds are shallow-rooted;
Suffer them now and they'll o'ergrow the garden
And choke the herbs for want of husbandry.

2 Henry VI 3.1.31–3

❊

Most subject is the fattest soil to weeds.

2 Henry IV 4.4.54

❊

Covering discretion with a coat of folly,
As gardeners do with ordure hide those roots
That shall first spring and be most delicate.

Henry V 2.4.38–40

Superfluous branches
We lop away, that bearing boughs may live.

Richard II 3.4.63–4

❧

Adam was a gardener.

2 Henry VI 4.2.126

❧

There is no ancient gentlemen but gardeners, ditchers,
and grave-makers – they hold up Adam's profession.

Hamlet 5.1.29–31

❧

Our bodies are gardens, to the which our wills are
gardeners.

Othello 1.3.322–3

Flowers

O Proserpina,
For the flowers now that, frighted, thou let'st fall
From Dis's waggon!

Winter's Tale 4.4.116–18

❀

What's in a name? That which we call a rose
By any other word would smell as sweet.

Romeo and Juliet 2.2.43–4

❀

The rose looks fair, but fairer we it deem
For that sweet odour which doth in it live.

Sonnet 54

A violet in the youth of primy nature,
Forward, not permanent, sweet, not lasting.

Hamlet 1.3.7–8

❈

For you, there's rosemary, and rue; these keep
Seeming and savour all the winter long.

Winter's Tale 4.4.74–5

❈

Sweets to the sweet.

Hamlet 5.1.241

❈

Fairies use flowers for their charactery.

Merry Wives of Windsor 5.5.73

Yet marked I where the bolt of Cupid fell:
It fell upon a little western flower,
Before milk-white, now purple with love's wound:
And maidens call it 'love-in-idleness'.

Midsummer Night's Dream 2.1.165–8

※

I know a bank where the wild thyme blows,
Where oxlips and the nodding violet grows,
Quite over-canopied with luscious woodbine,
With sweet musk-roses, and with eglantine.
There sleeps Titania sometime of the night,
Lulled in these flowers with dances and delight;
And there the snake throws her enamelled skin,
Weed wide enough to wrap a fairy in.

Midsummer Night's Dream 2.1.249–56

Over hill, over dale,
   Thorough bush, thorough briar,
Over park, over pale,
   Thorough flood, thorough fire,
I do wander everywhere,
Swifter than the moon's sphere;
And I serve the Fairy Queen,
To dew her orbs upon the green.
The cowslips tall her pensioners be,
In their gold coats spots you see;
Those be rubies, fairy favours,
In those freckles live their savours.
I must go seek some dew-drops here,
And hang a pearl in every cowslip's ear.

Midsummer Night's Dream 2.1.2–15

The summer's flower is to the summer sweet,
Though to itself it only live and die.

Sonnet 94

There's rosemary, that's for remembrance – pray you,
love, remember. And there is pansies, that's for thoughts
. . . There's fennel for you, and columbines. There's rue
for you. And here's some for me. We may call it herb
of grace a Sundays. You must wear your rue with a
difference. There's a daisy. I would give you some violets,
but they withered all when my father died.

Hamlet 4.5.173–5, 178–83

❧

There is a willow grows askant the brook
That shows his hoary leaves in the glassy stream.
Therewith fantastic garlands did she make
Of crow-flowers, nettles, daisies, and long purples,
That liberal shepherds give a grosser name,
But our cold maids do dead men's fingers call them.

Hamlet 4.7.166–71

Crowned with rank fumiter and furrow-weeds,
With burdocks, hemlock, nettles, cuckoo-flowers,
Darnel and all the idle weeds that grow
In our sustaining corn.

King Lear 4.4.3–6

❈

Fair flowers that are not gathered in their prime
Rot, and consume themselves in little time.

Venus and Adonis 131–2

❈

Feed him with apricocks and dewberries,
With purple grapes, green figs, and mulberries;
The honey-bags steal from the humble-bees,
And for night-tapers crop their waxen thighs,
And light them at the fiery glow-worms' eyes.

Midsummer Night's Dream 3.1.158–62

When I consider every thing that grows
Holds in perfection but a little moment;
That this huge stage presenteth nought but shows
Whereon the stars in secret influence comment;
When I perceive that men as plants increase,
Cheered and checked even by the self-same sky,
Vaunt in their youthful sap, at height decrease,
And wear their brave state out of memory:
Then the conceit of this inconstant stay
Sets you, most rich in youth, before my sight,
Where wasteful time debateth with decay
To change your day of youth to sullied night:
   And all in war with time for love of you
   As he takes from you, I engraft you new.

Sonnet 15